# THE NEXT LIFE

# Pat Boran

DEDALUS PRESS
DUBLIN, IRELAND

## ACKNOWLEDGEMENTS & THANKS

Acknowledgements are due to the editors and producers of the following journals in which a number of these poems, or versions of them, originally appeared: *Boulevard Magenta* (Irish Museum of Modern Art), *The Clifden Anthology, The Irish American Post, Link Up (Portlaoise), Migrating Minds, The Moth, New Hibernia Review, PoemCafe (Korea), Poetry Ireland Review, Poetry Salzburg, The SHOp, Smartish Pace* (USA), *Southword* online and *The Stinging Fly*. Poems also appeared in the following anthologies: *The Best of Irish Poetry* 2009, edited by Paul Perry, *Sunday Miscellany, A Selection from 2008–2011,* edited by Cliodhna Ní Anluain, *The Watchful Heart: A New Generation of Irish Poets* (2009), edited by Joan McBreen, *La Paume Ouverte: A Festschrift for Françoise Connolly,* edited by Theo Dorgan (2010), and *Windows Poetry Anthology 2012,* edited by Heather Brett and Noel Monahan. 'The Princess of Sorrows' appears in the forthcoming *Hartnett Echoing* anthology, edited by James Lawlor. Two of the poems included here first appeared in the 'New Poems' section of *New and Selected Poems* (2005/2007). A number of poems were first broadcast on the RTÉ Radio 1 programme *Sunday Miscellany* under the expert guidance of producer Clíodhna Ní Anluain.

Special thanks to Paula Meehan and Theo Dorgan for their careful reading of the manuscript and their sage advice. Sincere thanks, too, to Lawrence O'Shaughnessy, its patron, and to Thomas Dillon-Redshaw and James S. Rogers of the University of St. Thomas, St. Paul, MN, for the Lawrence O'Shaughnessy Award for Irish Poetry in 2008, and for their continued interest and encouragement since.

Thanks too to all the poets and translators who, on discovering my poem 'A Man is Only as Good' on the Poetry International web site some years ago, took the trouble to translate it into half a dozen languages and give it a new life online.

# COMHAIRLE CHONTAE ÁTHA CLIATH THEAS
## SOUTH DUBLIN COUNTY LIBRARIES
### COUNTY LIBRARY, TOWN CENTRE, TALLAGHT
*TO RENEW ANY ITEM TEL: 462 0073*
*OR ONLINE AT www.southdublinlibraries.ie*

Items should be returned on or before the last date below. Fines, as displayed in the Library, will be charged on overdue items.

First published in 2012
The Dedalus Press
13 Moyclare Road
Baldoyle
Dublin 13
Ireland

www.dedaluspress.com

ISBN 978 1 906614 55 3 (paperback)

Dedalus Press titles are represented in the UK by
Central Books, 99 Wallis Road, London E9 5LN
and in North America by Syracuse University Press, Inc.,
621 Skytop Road, Suite 110, Syracuse, New York 13244.

Cover painting: 'Passeggero fiammingo', oil on canvas,
60 x 80 cm, 2006 by Gaetano Tranchino
www.gaetanotranchino.it

The Dedalus Press receives financial assistance from
The Arts Council / An Chomhairle Ealaíon

# Contents

III

# IV

... a man sees death in things.
That is what it is to be a man.
— *Gilgamesh, A Verse Narrative* by Herbert Mason


Today is the tomorrow we were talking about yesterday.
— A favourite saying of my mother's

*for Lee and Luca*

**1**

# Worm Song

Articulated
servant of the plain truth
seldom stated,

part link, part chain,
serpent echo
in the slow lane

though sawn in half
on your journey
to the heart

of darkest matter. O lonely
shunting of the earth song
too low to sing; O hole

in the ring; O dull
but faithful sexton
of hallowed ground,

of growth and change,
pushing ahead
(again, and still again)

to where the sun
can never enter
though the rain seeps in—

O mindless worker,
blind muck-raker,
self-buried miner,

in your endless night
unmake all this, we pray,
to make it all alright.

# The Garden

Back in the back garden's light-dappled arbour
where the bees are like satellites
orbiting planets of fruit,

the uncut grass swaying, a radio playing
*The Last Rose of Summer, The Young Ones,*
*Only For You;*

no watch on my wrist, a twig in my fist,
my sights on a chain of black ants
advancing through space,

brazen but nervous, frantic but focused
on their final objective, the limit,
the summit, their aim;

in the hedge school of slumber at the back end of summer,
that blind spot the world overlooked
but us kids knew so well,

in the gap between trees, in the lapse between certainties,
held in suspense in the moment,
free in its spell.

## Snowman

No matter that we prayed
to God himself (father, son
and holy ghost), as well as half a dozen saints
we knew by name and some
odd talent or disfigurement—
the power to raise the dead,
to put out fires with their breath
or balance all night up a pole—
the meltdown came.

The head was first to go,
the belly lost a pound or two,
an eye came loose, the carrot nose
slipped an inch then disappeared
entirely overnight: perhaps a rat
or early bird had dragged it off.

Before we knew it
our snowman became snow-thing,
stooped and hunched, a drunk
in a dirty linen suit, a gatecrasher
who'd lost his way, forced to spend the night
outside alone. Who could love him any more?
Even the crozier that had made him seem
so wise last week — our own St Patrick —
lay now like a question mark at his feet.

# The Island

*for Bob Quinn*


Remote, solitary, its back to its neighbours,
facing instead the broad Atlantic and the dream
of a bright New World, that unkempt heap
of sand set down in our back yard by a builder

in the early 1970s became, the afternoon
he failed to show, our own small island: bays
and mountains, the major rivers, greys
instead of forty shades of green. Immune

to damp and cold, down on our knees
like the migrant workers of a generation before,
we laboured beyond nightfall until a door
in the darkness opened and saw us lifted clear

of our obsession. But who could sleep that night
leaving our small-but-perfect local wonder
with no one to defend it, alone there under
a cloud-marbled sky? Moonlight

flooding the house, I crept back down to check,
and found, to my astonishment, a fleet of snails,
like so many Norse or Spanish or Phoenician sails,
their glistening trails criss-crossing the hostile dark.

# Apple

*If you wish to make an apple pie from scratch,*
*you must first invent the universe.*
*— Carl Sagan*


Now, at last, with the volume down
and the stage curtains of the night drawn shut,
it's time to close in on this lone
still somehow strangely bright

fallen apple, since morning sat
here on the table, a glistening
keepsake, temptation's fruit,
for all the world a numinous thing:

the stalk's simple, perfect serif
rising from the wormhole navel;
the skin's luminous photograph
in three dimensions of the whole, scarcely plausible

history of time, the universe
to this moment — impossible to understand
yet simply expressed, the infinite eclipsed
by the tangible, by the close-at-hand.

# The Jeweller's Window

A hearse advances slowly up the street.
Only now do I notice the lowered blinds,
the shop signs turned to Closed, the lights
all off. Retreat

is quite impossible: in the entire world
there is not a single street in which the child
I am might be brought to turn
his back on this, though why

it is revealed to me, or what
it means, I'm sure I'll never know.
For years I'll stand before this window
where the watches tremble, hesitate, but never stop.

# Green Mill Lane

*for John Dunne*


Crossing over the hump backed bridge
where the old mill my father kept
as a lock-up used to stand, I see him
everywhere still. Not ten steps
ahead of me, he's there on his knees,
lifting masonry back into place
in a weeping drystone wall, bent in half
to gather litter, or tipping a branch
into the ditch with the toe of his boot,
a man at his ease clearing a path
for the strangers who follow us, driving past
with barely so much as a glance, or for me
caught yet again in the amber of memory —
the sun going down, the stream running clear,
and, as they never did in his time,
those rust-bucket wheels turning free.

# Space Travel

In my school friend's back yard,
among the crates and silver kegs of beer
I never saw the promised corpse.

But on one occasion I recall,
fascinated by their gleaming hearse
under a soft fall of rain, we snuck

into the family workshop. *Keegan & Sons,*
the signboard proclaimed, *Publicans
& Undertakers.* We were ten,

but out there in that dim-lit space,
made brave by laughter we clambered in
and stood, in silence, side by side,

in two open coffins, rough-planed and propped
against a wall. Whole minutes passed,
neither of us wanting to be the one to break

the spell. Now thirty years have gone,
and I'm home to take my first ever drink
in the family pub, at his father's wake.



*Biers & spirits;* stiff ones and stiffs ...
The old jokes come back to haunt
at every return or passing visit.

The old doubts, too. Is that how it was?
Did we go, or only dream we could?
Yet another adventure never begun ...

Last night on my way up town
I stopped to stare into that off-street darkness,
and wondered how we would have looked

back then, back there, had either one
of our now late fathers happened past —
two small-town youngsters with time on their hands,

stood on the launch pad like astronauts,
ready for the journey to a better world,
schoolbags heavy with oxygen on our backs.

# The Reed Bed

The reeds that grew along the banks
of my first real love, the local stream,
generations back were prized

for basket weaving, mats and thatch
durable and waterproof
as any roof of slate or tile

a man might raise above his head.
Reed paper, it is said,
sufficed when better stuff proved scarce,

and the nibs of pens, themselves from reeds,
made reed-upon-reed the perfect match —
nothing between the two but air.

These last few nights, reeds everywhere
when I close my eyes and start to drift,
home after years in the reed bed

of childhood, carried aloft
to where reeds are plaintive in the breeze,
trout and minnow have not yet lost

their struggle to survive, and men on the run,
hidden in shallows till the bloodhounds pass,
peaceful as infants breathe through hollow reeds.

# Faith

Pushed out of the boat, my father
like so many of his siblings learned to swim
out of necessity. He'd seen, no doubt,
a sack of cats go down into the same

Dinin River, and might well have dreamed
the blackness at the far end of that string
of beads, those seeds of air that rose
to bloom and blossom on the water's skin.

And perhaps that helped. More likely though,
fear moved faster through his veins
than any conscious thought, and he was
kicking water, grasping, gulping air

almost before he knew he'd been pushed in,
*his* father extending from that small craft
an arm or splintered oar with which
to fish him out, still gasping, into an ark.

## Toad

A toad on the footpath,
first toad I've seen
anywhere in years. Like a cross
between a sumo wrestler and a kid
I knew in school, always
stopping in mid-stride, crouching down
as if to relieve himself, and then,
for no clear reason, bursting into tears.

Probably his father beat him
before he left. Probably the kid
never felt far enough out of the reach
of those big fists, toad-skin rough.
Or that's how I pictured it,
and picture him now, toad boy
long since grown but squatting somewhere
on a glistening path, his green-brown eyes
full of emptiness, his face
alien with grief.

## Provisional

When a youngster dies,
the whole town comes to a halt.
They cry in the street,
in the queue at the supermarket,
they cry holding hands at school.
They cry who have felt
death move among them,
rattling the pens in a pencil case,
turning the pages of a textbook
with that icy breath.

How else could it be
in a town so small
the priest plays golf with the father,
the gaunt gravedigger
is the mother's second cousin (once removed),
and his lock-jawed son —
the first on the scene, as it happens —
only two years before
himself almost perished
on this same stretch of road
they shuffle up now,

wind kicking dust in their faces,
sending their hats into orbit
like souls that swoop and swerve
forever out of reach.

# Honeysuckle

*for Ron Houchin*

He took the back roads and drove for hours
till the sky was the puddle of stars he had lost
in his boyhood and never bothered to miss
before now, the night of his 50th birthday,
his parents and neighbours long dead, the old house
bulldozed out of existence, the pond
in-filled and covered with tarmac, a stop sign
where a scarecrow once stood, the road falling off
into the distance, and only the stars
still familiar, still reliable, and that scent in the dark
he called, then and still, honeysuckle.

## 'Up the Road'

Up the road and around the bend,
beyond the oak tree or the old shed
where Fionn MacCumhaill spent a night
or we holed up one evening in the yellow light

of a thunderstorm, at the edge of town
where trucks change gear, where sense breaks down
and the whole broke country was showing off its veins
to the needle of the Lord, that's the place

you'll dream about, you're reaching towards
when darkness flares, when you choke on words
in the middle of nowhere, the place you'll miss
when the next life begins and you look back on this.

# Corrie Lake, Gorteenameale, Slieve Bloom Mountains

*for Kevin Flanagan*


Some say it might have been a meteorite,
others that there must have been a cult
drawn to these mountains, their bright
occasional flowers, the dark rough

texture of the peat. Either way,
even here, so far up from the towns
and lowland villages, the daily trade
of life and death, this perfectly round

iris of water, this unexplained lake,
is a living window. Beside it you feel
the presence of the lost, the late,
the disappeared. The great wheel

of time seems to have a hub,
a point around which past and future
turn. A man out with his dog
becomes a pilgrim, and the distant river

and the paths beyond are signs
in some ancient language, predating words.
So whether it was dug out by a line
of men with shovels, climbing through the furze

of the lower hills, emerging into sky as clear
as ocean, or whether one great blast
of cosmic power found its endpoint here,
it makes no difference. This might be the last

limpid eye of water left on earth
or the first of a new era to begin
at any moment. A kind of rebirth
occurs the very instant you look in.

# Matchbox Wheels

*i.m. Billy Brophy*

From Stradbally he came — half a day's ride
on our high nellies — in a small case
two or three dozen matchbox trays
we'd never see again in the same light.
One tray slotting neatly into the next,
his careful step-by-step progression turned
in on itself until the last and the first
completed the circle, and he taped them down.
Those matchbox wheels, we played with them for days,
an idea whose time had at long last come
to our sleepy, landlocked, midland town,
our ancient creaking vessel of a home
where two wonders arrived that same afternoon,
the Renaissance and the Industrial Revolution.

# Coal

My father's people died for it, one breath at a time,
this sinister cousin of diamond, this blackest of sheep,
hewn from the deep space of earth, the cliff face of night,
the dark matter all the while under their feet.

Down on their bellies, like babies, sons trailing fathers
through chambers half-flooded by seepage and by sweat,
through panics of vermin, pockets of breathable air,
deeper than burial, into the very neighbourhood of death

and beyond they crawled; and they didn't go alone
but with the prayers of those they left above
shallow-breathing to watch them setting out at dawn,
the men whose shadows dusk would gather home.

The mines are long since closed, the channels inundated.
Coal now comes from some underworld a world away.
The engine of empire, cold and alien as ever
it remains as much a mystery today

as when I held it for the first time in my hand,
a small boy sensing the story of his tribe,
his blood; asteroid-tough, history and memory compressed
into one, the darkness brought into the light.

# Milk Bottles

Decades since I heard it last,
this early morning tell-tale clink-
clink of glass bottles set
gently in place on the front step.

And wondering if absence might explain
its hold on me, I'm on my feet
to draw back the curtains and, right enough,
glimpse through the half-mist of Main Street

stretching into life below
the open-backed, wire-crate stacked
fabled milk van pulling off
like an emigrant ship, and there on deck

one blue tit passenger who must start from scratch
on whichever blessed island he finds himself.

# Prison Visit

Lovers, losers, villains,
the town is out
tonight to watch
a perfect sunset
hesitate over the prison.

Who do we gaol?
The citizens who fail us?
The citizens we fail?

Love is powerful
but life is tough.
In the mud
behind the prison wall —
toy handcuffs.

**II**

# String

It starts with string,
that familiar, wholly alien thing
that coils and turns on itself
like a puzzle, like drizzle
making shapes on glass. I write
as fast as I can, the images
blaze past; but it's late, and I cannot keep up.

Next morning I step out into a garden
of sunshine and birds, a breeze
replacing the storm winds, a morning so bright
I wish I could sing, but the memory of string
sings stronger, coiling and turning,
flicking its tail, and my failure
to grasp what it hints at is binding.

Since then, nothing at all. The year grows
cold in my hands. Once fresh with dew
the leaves are already falling
home into earth, parting with flesh,
their stems the last remaining
elements, part punctuation, part —*ah!*—
puzzling alphabet of string.

# The Princess of Sorrows

*i.m. Michael Hartnett*


The Princess of Sorrows blames herself
and cannot disguise it. For too long now
she has sat on this footpath and no longer knows
the way home. In the hostel she feels
she will one day be invisible, even to herself.
On nights like this only a doorway
seems solid. So five nights a week
she comes to sit here, her head to one side,
as though the fall or the blow
that has scarred her nose since yesterday
had snapped her neck. Rag-doll princess,
inner child of the inner city
set adrift, I touch your sleeve,
I drop a note in your paper cup;
I greet you in English, in Irish, in Greek,
or something that sounds like Greek; I speak
Lorca's Spanish, the Latin of Catullus,
two or three words of Romanian learned
one night in a bar from two drunken thieves
equally lost ... And then it ends, passes,
the dance that's inside me, and I tip
the tip of my cap, clicking my heels
like poetry's Fred Astaire, and bow
low before you in inherited shame
at having so little to offer you here
on this Baggot Street night, in this Baggot Street rain,
where the cars flow past in a river of lights,
and we are not strangers, not any more,
but the Princess of Sorrows and Hartnett the poet,
each of us homeless in every language known.

## 'Dream of the Sparrow Morning'

Dream of the Sparrow Morning:
a line from some imagined Chinese poem,

a fragment of wisdom,
blurred by translation,

or something glanced at, flicked past
in a bookshop somewhere
years ago,

and forgotten
until now,

comes back to you,
come back *for* you,

wakes just before you do
in the dawn light,
to whisper in your ear.

And the more you think on it,
puzzle over it,
the more the phrase
professes no great
interest in meaning.

Dream of the Sparrow Morning:
five words having found each other,
a burst of colour on a hillside field,
the wild flowers of language.

And yet, now, watch as they lend themselves,
title-like, to everything you see:

your shirt and jeans draped over the chair,
your shoes standing by to useless attention,
your curled-up wristwatch on the bedside table,
foetal, like you and, like you, blank in the early light.

Dream of the Sparrow: Morning.

Dream of the Sparrow-Morning.

Or, my favourite:
Dream of the Sparrow (comma) Morning,
an exhortation, a prayer of breath,
a call for this bright morning to produce
that brown-grey plump-breasted short-tailed bird
whom Sappho imagined
drawing Aphrodite's chariot
across the heavens.

So, Dream of the Sparrow, Morning,
the soft landing of that comma
somehow perfect,
(the happy accident of its worm-like appearance)
as you draw the curtains this morning to reveal
the lawn outside and find the sparrows
already settled in, all business,
dreamt up by morning, conjured by it,
and making the most of the light.

# Touchdown

*(The Brent Geese return to Bull Island)*


Bay, open bay, spread out below
the cloud banks, cloud-dappled, drenched
in greens and greys, scarred
by the sudden and gradual
in equal parts, but firm;

one foot-sized expanse of it,
and another beside it shimmering,
that waits for the fall of shadow,
the relaxing of muscles, the folding
of wing and reach, the dip
and careful drift down into touch
and sodden

solidity of place — the screech
of other selves, echoing of hunger,
and the ache, the sheer
collective ache, after
so much longing, so much
of nothing else to depend on
but open air.

# Skipping

With the intensity of a character in a fairytale
a small girl skips in the street
outside our house. For most of the morning
she has been there, skipping and singing to herself,
now with a friend, now with a whole gang of friends,
now on her own. Each time the rope comes round
she lifts herself up out of her shadow
with just a flick of her toes,
and whether friends chant some muddled rhyme
no small girl ever really understands
or worries much about,
or whether the ice-cream van goes by,
slows down, tinkling its promise,
on she goes, skipping and leaving the world
over and over, loving
the weight of herself, her weightlessness,
the swoosh of the rope.

# Easter

Easter morning, first light
through the window, first-second-third-fourth birds
already up and in place to sing
their small but crucial parts in the mystery.

No work today. Today
the observed routine of quiet,
the ticking clock granted centre stage,
the cold shock and sudden cascade
of water from the tap once more
miraculous. I splash
and dry my face, slide back
the back door and step slowly out —
into existence, it feels like,
all the stars of the universe
dimmed into second place
by our local wonder.

A mug of coffee warm in my hands,
sunlight falling on my face,
beyond the garden and across the bay
the mountains seem to settle into themselves
as if a circus master were folding up his tents
before moving on to the next too-busy town.

## Corner Boys

The toughest man in town is now a granddad,
and every morning, his teenage daughter back
at secondary school, the local dogs
set free to chase each other through the park,

a vision in tattoos and knee-length shorts —
half pirate, half fairground muscleman —
he's out to push a Dora the Explorer pram
the length of the terrace, stopping to complain

about his lot, the dogs, the litter everywhere,
to pick a broken bottle off the road
and chuck it in a bin, and, now and then,
to stand his ground and share a grim-faced joke

with another crew-cut granddad like himself,
thirty years ago his mortal foe,
the pair of them like boxers squaring up,
comparing snapshots on their mobile phones.

## Let's Die

'Let's die,' I say to my kids,
Lee aged five, Luca not yet three,
and under an August blanket of sun
we stretch out in the grass on a hill
to listen to the sea just below
drawing close, pulling back,
or to the sheep all around us
crunching their way down towards earth.

'Do you love the clouds, Dada?'
'Do you love the Pink Panther?'
and 'Will you stay with us for ever?'
to which I reply, without hesitation,
Yes, Yes and Yes again,
knowing that as long as we lie here
everything is possible, that any of the paths
up ahead might lead anywhere
but still, just in time, back home.

Like me, sometimes they act too much,
filling the available space and time
with fuss and noise and argument,
but up here, overlooking the landscape,
the seascape, of their lives, on this hill
they like to play this game, to lie
together and together to die
which, in their children's language, means
less to expire or to cease
than to switch to Super Attention Mode,
to prepare for travel, to strap oneself
into the booster seat and wait and wait

for the gradual but inexorable lift
up and off and out into motion.

For my two boys, things are only
recently made flesh, made mortal—
our uprooted palm tree, two goldfish,
the bird a neighbour's cat brought down
last week—and they are almost holy
with this knowledge. 'Let's die now,
then let's go home for tea,' Lee says,
putting into words as best he can
the sea's helpless love affair with the land.

## Goðafoss (Waterfall of the Gods, Iceland)

*for Caitriona O'Reilly*


After we had lost everything,
after we had stared into the abyss
and saw nothing we recognised as human
or on a human scale —

the glacier in the distance, sheets of ice
overlapping sheets of ice, the valley
broken open like a wound —

cold in our bones and ice-spray in our faces,
we started up those steps
cut into rock, lifted
by the hands of absent strangers
to a place where we could be ourselves again.

# Learning to Dive

The boy who is learning to dive
has a lot on his mind:

how to place
his unfamiliar, disobeying feet
on the slippery rungs;

how to straighten himself and walk
the length of the board
without glancing down;

how to stand, to extend
his arms straight ahead, as the other boys do,
without wavering;

how to cancel the height,
the shake in his legs,
once more how to breathe.

But while he stands there and the water stills,
from out of nowhere a kid half his size
goes charging past

to pedal pedal pedal in empty air,
before dropping through into the target
of his own reflection. Resounding cheers,

upon which the older boy gives up,
surrenders to something somewhere
beyond his control,

and at last steps clear
of the board to fall
away into the rapturous applause

of water, each glistening drop
a medal struck to honour his courage,
the triumph of his simply letting go.

# The Apple Tree

We bought it in the supermarket,
that flap-ended flexing limb of wood,
believing ourselves its liberators,
like blacked-up intruders who release
laboratory rats, setting off for home,
the thing stretched over the back seat
a tree in name alone, a patient
in the ambulance the car had become,
the city we passed through a landscape now
of concrete and steel, towers of glass
blankly watching as we blazed past.

At home we unwrapped and washed it slowly,
put it in a tub the kids packed
with compost, twigs and sympathetic magic —
a plastic soldier, some candies, small stones —
stroking the few wan leaves. Inside a week
new shoots appeared, a lifeless knot
puckered, stuck its tongue out, broke
into white flower. We laughed at our luck:
the dream of fruit, so far from Eden.

And when that first apple at last appeared
from behind a leaf — the first and last
as it transpired, like an only child —
it was as though the sun had singled out
our small back yard, that one dull tub
and sickly tree for special favour,
a starring role in the experiment of life.

# The Fox

The fox came back, the bowl of scraps we'd left
as darkness fell licked clean
and on its side, the only sign she'd been
and gone while our small party slept

just feet away. In our pop-up dome,
by day a credible playhouse,
with dusk a thing of string and hope
shadow-insects struck like a slack drum,

we'd drifted off. Or some of us had.
For I lay awake listening for hours
in that moon-milk light — fox-time

as I think of it now — my two cub scouts
breathing in unison, peace in the land,
that makeshift den warmed by their small flames.

## Lullaby

Day must make its peace with night,
the sky cloud over that was bright,
the sea-shells empty that once were white with spray.

The dark is deep, and overhead
starlight hangs on by a thread.
But sleep now, love, a thread is all it takes.

# Lawnmower Man

Midway along a trench of grass
the lawnmower dies. A breeze
nudges the grassheads;
the metal casing ticks and cools,
imitating life. Perched
on the garden slide, the kids look on
in silence, and I become
before their eyes
the grandfather I never knew,
his old mule fallen to its knees
in a field where God
has turned up the volume
of the smallest things:
birdsong, the shift of grass-
stalk against stalk, middle age's
first appearance in the play
these puzzled standstill moments,
those whisperings off stage.

# A Dog

*for Paula and Theo*

A dog is a judge.
You cannot lie to a dog.
Even when you do not speak
a dog can hear you.

Like the house you grew up in,
or the concrete shed
on the windy side of school,
dogs have no time
for who you think you are
or plan to become.
They exist in the world
of the moment.
Hours, days and years
mean nothing to a dog.

Like that overgrown plant
out the back, or the shirt
upstairs still in its Christmas wrapping
seven months on, a dog
is always waiting
for your return.

Then it's the soul of the universe,
its eyes are twin black holes
drawing in and pouring out
primordial stuff. Hearts
are broken and remade
with one look from a dog.

And there is nothing in its power
a dog would not do, if it could,
for the one who shows it kindness,
stick-chasing and dancing,
lifting the regal paw, melting
like slush over the kitchen floor
to sleep the one-eye-open
finding-the-right-position-still
sleep of the just.

Yet it is one of the great sorrows
with which we humans must contend
that dogs can report so little
though they see so much.

What we would know
of the world, of existence itself,
if only we could converse with them,
these friends who learned to bark
to assuage our loneliness,
these damp-smelling angels
who suffer our moods and our scoldings
and still, in the end —
the table cleared and lights turned off —
who lead us out one final time
to stand in the darkness
and wait, looking up
like shepherds beneath
the canopy of the stars.

## That Pain

that comes and goes in the lower right,
the lower left; that stabs and throbs
and burns and leaves then comes again
and, at night, again;

that tight almost white vibration
in the ear; that string of sound
that ties you up and down, that binds
and won't let go; that slow
withering irritation; the deep
plunge in the heart, the steep
and sudden fall-off from the shelf
of stand-up, stand-still,
face-front, eyes-to-the-sky
persistence;

that sense of something
missing, something broken,
something killed;

that nothing good or willed: that sudden
drop in the surge of the blood, that
gasping for breath or grasping for support,
that impulse for fight
or flight, that fright —

that's when you vow to live.

## 'Girl Gardening'

*"nuestro amor / es / terrestre"*
— *Pablo Neruda*

From this park bench I watch you on your knees
in the earth, head down, utterly intent
on your morning's work as the lightest breeze
flits between one small clutch of plants

and another. These past few days
you remind me more and more
of the girl in that Neruda poem whose name
I borrow now for this, as though

the world of all our brittle part-existences
were somehow stitched together after all
by the thread of chance, the distances
between us bridged by the tumble

of a book off a shelf, the accident
of a page fallen open. Our love,
the great poet had it, is *"terrestre"* — of the earth,
earthly, earth-dependent? — the glove

of translation a far-from-perfect fit.
And yet the meaning feels close by, as it was
a week ago when, coming here to sit
and read like this, some sudden noise

stopped me in my tracks and I turned to see
a cyclist meet his fate head on, slow motion
in retrospect but in the living stream
of time a thing completed in a moment,

the horror hidden by his lycra suit,
the hi-tech helmet that crowned his startled face.
In shock, trembling, I came in here and saw you
on your knees as every work-day, making space —

a queen who moves among us, sometimes stands
to survey the task, then carries on as before,
sifting and folding earth in earth-caked hands,
following the example of the humble worm

that takes whatever's given without complaint,
grass or clay, dead flowers, resilient weeds,
with little to mark those moments when the lights change
but the blessing of a million stirring leaves.

## Haiku

First day back at work,
muttering, dragging his feet—
the method actor.

# The Inverse Wave

He recorded every sound in the town,
the river, half full, the kids
in afternoon playgrounds, the fool
stood out on the street to sing,
the believers and all of the certain doomed
driving to work, eating their take-outs,
beached in the mid-summer heat. All of it,
all of them. And late one night he made
a digital negative, an inverse wave
which the following evening he broadcast so loud
on his stereo (driving around
with the windows rolled down and the volume up full)
that its sound cancelled out the originals
and everything went still:
the factories, the traffic,
the games and the arguments,
the inside and out,
the known world's perfect din and constant roar,
until all that was left was two lovers
in darkness, whispering together
words never uttered before.

**III**

# The Poet's Return

Royal Highness, Noble Lord,
I have come back from far beyond
the borderlands, from nameless places
stranger than any here have known,

to bring you some small gift or token,
as much as I could hope to take
and carry with me when all about
were broken, wandering blind and lame.

In a forest, in the topmost branches
of a giant, unfamiliar tree,
I glimpsed a bird, a tiny creature
unlike any I have ever seen.

Your armies? Butchered where they slept.
Your generals? Dead, half-dead, enslaved.
The cities we thought laid waste? My Liege,
laden with gold they are readying for war again.

But, Sire, I beg you, hear my words:
in that tree that night, such music, such a bird ...

## 'Because of Some Killings'

'Because of some killings',
because of famine in the land,
because of grief, madness, revenge,
a new king, an old enemy returned ...

Following an argument or dream,
on a whim, to settle a wager,
in error, by accident, en route
to pastures new, the future

is suddenly upon us, the track home
obscured by trees, the ground
turns soft, heavy, and somewhere close
the baying of the bounty hunter's hounds.

# During the War

We met, fell in love, set up home,
while the world prepared for war.
As battleships took up positions off the coast,
we began to clear the spare room.

They cut power lines, we laid carpet.
They jammed radio signals, we whistled to ourselves,
lifted floorboards, stripped paint and paper,
and each night fell into bed exhausted,
content with these glimpses
of a better world to come.

The day the first bombs fell on Baghdad,
we finished what would be the nursery,
imagining the progress of tiny feet
as the stretcher-bearers set off
into a whirlwind of dust.

And a few years later, on the very day
six schoolkids died in Sadr city,
their school ripped open by a bomb that left
a hole in the road six feet deep,

we went to the zoo, our first big outing,
stopping before the well-kept cages,
waving at the animals, pulling faces,
trying out the noises we took to be their words.

## 'A Man is Only as Good'

A man is only as good
as what he says to a dog
when he has to get up out of bed
in the middle of a wintry night
because some damned dog has been barking;

and he goes and opens the door
in his vest and boxer shorts
and there on the pock-marked wasteground
called a playing field out front
he finds the mutt with one paw

raised in expectation
and an expression that says Thank God
for a minute there I thought
there was no one awake but me
in this goddamned town.

## The Homeless

When the homeless left town
the citizens were delighted. The story was
that one old bum had seen the irony
of always sleeping in the same damp doorway,
of being in it, as it were, at home.

So as one they rolled their stinking blankets
and left. People gave them money, food,
genuine good wishes. A man
drove a bus free of charge
to the edge of town.

In the schools
children sang and waved and small ones
cried as busloads disappeared from view
like emigrant ships.
                              Within a week
new homeless started showing up,
who knows where from. First a man
sat down on a park bench
and feel asleep. Across the street
Police observed him
from an unmarked car. Two teenage girls
entered a department store
and refused to leave, warming themselves
on a heater in the foyer
in full view.
                              Within the hour
a child had been observed
sitting on the steps of the Public Library
holding a sign that read: SPARE CHANGE, PLEASE,

his paper cup advertising (and this, I think,
hurt more than all the other disappointments)
a restaurant in the next town up the road.

# Revenge

Lear went mad, Heathcliff prowled the moors,
and the militants built home-made bombs in sheds
identical to ours: old rusted tools
hanging from the beams, an ancient bicycle
half buried under bags and bric-à-brac,
and, on a bench, covered with a hessian sac,
enough fire power to take a child's face off.
*Blow winds and crack your cheeks...* We read that
again and again, as if somehow the words
through repetition alone would start to make sense.

# Intruder

He doesn't recognise me, this scrawny kid
a few summers back still mowing lawns
for pocket money, now suddenly reborn
as the local tearaway, his shaved head
exposed in the full-moon beam of my flashlight
to the rear of the house, the world fast asleep,
autumn yet, by a thread, by the skin of its teeth.

'Looking for my ball,' he says, matter of fact,
defiant, in his hand, half on show,
a bat or something heavier proposing
the alternatives. 'At this hour?' I laugh
and stand my ground, part fool, part sage,
wondering what else might lie within reach
in the inky dark that floods the moment's page.

He sniffs, shifts uneasily, never looks away.
It's as though he's faced me a dozen times before,
the drunken father staggering through the door
at closing time, fists raised, shouting obscenities
for the whole estate to hear. Silence. A grunt,
then he's over the six-foot wall in a judder
of branches and shadows, less like a creature

fleeing than a creature in flight, the night air
electric, the garden alert to the brim
of the fence posts, the cap-stones, the tendrils of clematis
inching up through the stars …
                                        In the flickering dark
I wait for the echo of footsteps retreating,
hear nothing at all. Instead, like a picture

taken from orbit, there's us here, this youngster
and my middle-aged self, two figures bent double,
catching our breaths, one stood in grass
neatly trimmed, the other in splinters of glass
from a dangling street-lamp, hearts pumping
faster than lovers', the wall here between us
ungiving (yes), alien (surely), and cold to the touch —
not living (of course) and yet somehow bristling with
    gooseflesh.

## The Alternative Tour of Ireland

And this, the tour guide says, is the roundabout
where that Roma family famously camped out
a few years back, the eye
of the cyclone then, election posters
spread out on the ground for mattresses,
commuters blazing past, gazing off
to where the latest hyperstore
was even then beginning to take shape —
that aircraft hangar of dreams. Some wrote
to local TDs, asking what it all meant,
while others, like myself, slowed down,
but in the end drove reluctantly on —
what else could we do? The make-shift tents,
the washing hung out like so many flags
of surrender ... And then, days later,
everything cleaned up,
nothing at all to be seen
but a man's discarded undershirt
snagged on a bush, a hole in its heart
and a long cane of thorns pushing through.

# Guilt

Only the guilty deny their crimes
with such composure, rising to find
the white vans parked on the lawn outside,
the grim-faced reporters with their notebooks
    and satellite phones.

Only the guilty always look their best,
neatly coiffed, impeccably dressed,
flashbulbs igniting around their heads
like angels around the tonsures of the gods.

To the loyal supporters gathered back home,
or the former colleagues long since flown
to some 'more enlightened' taxation zone,
only the guilty wave with such steady hands.

They alone manage the hearty meal
on the day of the hearing, endure the ordeal
with exemplary patience, and are back at the wheel
of that ninety-grand Jag for a victory lap of the town

as the new unemployed come staggering home,
exhausted, dejected, powerless as drones,
the burden of worry dragging them down
and the urge to confess when they so much as glance
    in a mirror.

# Bargain Hunter

Talk-box, squawk-box ... The other day
I found an antique wireless
in a local jumble sale,

the lacquer scarred, the dial stiff
and grating, the entrails scarcely contained
by the duct tape plastered across the back.

But could it work? I turned a knob:
a valve glowed orange, a whooshing noise
conjured the void, then a male voice spoke

clear and authoritative, not the words
I'd half-expected ("...*consequently*
*this country is at war ...*") but instead

"*Ireland returns to world markets,*
*Taoiseach rules out default on bonds,*
*Health service closures cripple nation.*"

I turned it off, and tried a helmet on.

# Shipwrecked

It used to be simple:
shipwrecked, you turned the boat over
and started from scratch,

your new home the nave
of a church, its prow pointing back
over the ocean

towards your previous life.
You lived with the loss,
did what you could, carried on.

You learned from mistakes,
your foolish belief
in the big talk of others;

you built things from bits
and from bones, what the sea offered up.
Now you're convinced

every sail is your saviour,
every noise is a plane
crossing the vastness of ocean

over and back, all these years later
still searching for you, the sole
survivor, waiting to tell them precisely

where it all went so wrong.

# Immigrants Open Shops

*i.m. Sargon Boulus, Iraqi poet (1944 – 2007)*

Immigrants open shops, Sargon says.
In countries where they take in refugees,
that's what they do, they open shops.
To sell something, there's no real need to speak;

someone enters, points at 'this and that'
or finds what he wants on a shelf,
and all you need is half a dozen words
to serve him, 'yes', 'no', 'seven', 'Euros', 'ten' —

he's counting fingers — words a fool can master
in a morning, could be singing in two days,
and maybe 'thank you', or 'see you tomorrow'.
Immigrants, they open shops, Sargon says.


Immigrants open shops, Sargon says,
a teenaged girl perched high on a stool
happy to try the few new words she's learned
after her first week in the local school.

But when they pass through the bead curtains
into the back room, when they step back from the till,
or when friends or family drop by for a taste
of the old country, it's the old language still:

a newspaper lying open on a table,
the TV always on on the high shelf
making the drunk who stumbles in by accident
wonder if he's the immigrant here himself.

Immigrants open shops, Sargon says,
eight years ago already, hard to believe,
the troops back then still gathering on the border
of the homeland he hadn't seen in twenty years.

'One for the road?' he asks. I shrug: 'Why not?
As my mother says, we'll be a long time dead.'
Sargon smiles: 'I'll remember that, my friend,'
but he's far away this evening, lost in himself,

gazing out into our tidy garden
through his pale reflection in the glass,
a nervous shopkeeper as night approaches
hearing ominous voices in the dark.

## 'Love, if you wake in the night'

*for Raffaela*


Love, if you wake in the night
to hear a door open,

if a stairboard should creak,
the kettle growl into life,

or, upright in bed,
if you should sense down below you

the murmur of voices,
a long drawn-out, lonely sigh,

don't be afraid, no need to fret,
turn back to sleep,

that's only me
the resident ghost of the place,

making the most
of the five-in-the-morning feel

of our home being carried
by dream through the darkness of space.

What can I tell you?
Along with the sweetness and light

the day we were married
ten years back you signed up for this

benevolent haunting, this hunting
through shadows and signs,

this backyard astronomy,
this science of half-finished lists

where a tune that I heard years ago,
a storm off at sea

or a breeze through a keyhole
can keep me up puzzling till dawn,

until light fills the windows,
a stair creaks, and you reappear,

and at last I can see why I've waited
but the words are all gone.

## Absence

Slipping into bed
just now, your hair tickled me.
I wish you were here.

# Enemies

Boys who were once our enemies
at last become our friends.
How little it takes, a smile or nod,
a friendly word, and all that hurt's

undone. We've seen
time erase whole kingdoms,
wipe out every trace
of great dictators and their victims,

but who'd have guessed
as we faced each other
all those years ago
across dancehall floors

a joke might bridge the divide,
a handshake make all the difference,
or that in no time at all we'd be feeling
each other's pain,

waking like this
in the dead of the night,
the name on our lips for once
neither threat nor supplication.

# September 11th, 2011

1.

Horror finds us out
        in places it forever
draws us back to. That afternoon

it was a beach in Sicily,
        surrounded by friends and family,
the eve of what would be

our wedding day — the horror
        those trembling, grainy pictures
beamed around the world:

the blue skies, the planes
        slicing through the towers,
the towers so utterly impassive

then falling in slow motion,
        exhaling dust-clouds
like underwater creatures

exhaling ink.


2.

Good fortune
        is crucial in our lives,
my meeting you, the love

that grew to claim us.
      I thought it then
and that next afternoon

emerging from the darkness
      into blinding light,
the shock of applause,

and rice-grains falling on our heads.


3.

Ten years later on a Dublin stage
      I recall the shell-shocked feelings
of those first few hours:

the fear, the guilt, the sense
      that even at such a distance
we too were there.

Later, the house-lights up,
      the audience starts to leave
and a man I know comes towards me

like some desert storm, head down,
      fists clenched, vein
bulging in his neck, his loved ones

behind him, embarrassed
      or afraid. He ignores
my outstretched hand, instead

accusing me through gritted teeth:
        "You're an apologist
for the American global war machine".

I lean in closer, certain
        I can't heard him right. "They got,"
he snarls, "what they deserved."

And I want to strike him then,
        wish he'd strike me first —
the father of my friend, his eyes

of fire, his flesh of dust.


4.


Jamaicans, Japanese, Jordanians,
        lone victims from Belgium and Belarus,
the Ivory Coast and Venezuela,

citizens of 90 sovereign states
        (our own among them),
Christians, Muslims, Jews,

two three-year old toddlers,
        and an eighty-year-old from Maine
on his first interstate flight,

almost three thousand lives
        ended in a morning to illustrate
nothing that the poor

of Baghdad or Kandahar
        or a hundred other cursed places
don't already know:

that the murdered are not consoled
        by yet more murders,
that vampires alone repeat

the lie of revenge. "They got ..."


5.

"... what they deserved." Six months on
        I cannot let it go. Tonight
I close my eyes and see

his eyes before me, their furious
        certainty, and what I face
is not a man who steps out

bravely from the crowd
        but one whose deeds
obscure the very cause he would espouse,

the lights all on, his family
        gathered there around him,
cowering, faces covered

against the shrapnel of his love.

# Fairouz

*Siracusa, August 2012*

Dust lifts and falls in an empty street,
dogs sleep in shadow, and overhead
from an open window a voice drifts free,
at first scarcely audible, the slow motion dance
of rapture and longing, hope and despair;
and now the heartbreak that is Fairouz is everywhere.

No greater voice has emerged to sing
the hurt of the world, in love or war,
here on a backstreet where Europe begins
or at home in Beirut, her bloodied flower,
where this afternoon the airwaves again
carry the healing syllables of her pain.

All trembling longing, full of the doubt
that is love, and the heart's brief hope,
hers is the voice of a lover returned
under cover of nightfall, come now on tiptoe,
her breath in your ear, on the nape of your neck,
the rhythm insistent, mesmeric, the melody
lifting you clear of the horrors men do
by their failure to listen, to put difference aside,
and, whatever the cost, *to lay down their weapons
and apologize.* *

* *The words of the Syrian poet Nizar Qabbani who once suggested the
singer's voice had the power to persuade men to turn away from
violence.*

76

**IV**

## 'Cut grass, clear skies'

Cut grass, clear skies, almond-
scented air, and the fine hair
on your forearm glistening.

I know a man who sings
each morning of such found
miracles, a man who cares

too much perhaps for the things
that get him nowhere
though they make his world go round.

Yet how else to begin
this inventory, this slow grounding,
this morning prayer.

## The Plan

On the beach at Malahide
the young couple playing some strange game
with sticks and tape, pacing back and forth
and back again — no ball in sight — turn out to be

mapping out the house they plan to build,
its walls and doorways inscribed in wet sand,
moving from imagined room to room
beneath the setting sun, the rising moon.

## The Nurse

The nurse comes out and tells the boy, *I'm sorry.*
It seems to take all her energy to lift
her slender arm, to place her open palm
gently on the youngster's shoulder, as if to steady

both of them. Perhaps this is her first time
to cross this gap, no watch or jewellery,
her hair tied back, her eyes salt-stung as if
she swam to stand here trembling in the light.

## The Distance

Empty. Almost cold.
As if fear were our only reason
for standing still,

we watched, like people on a bridge,
for what the river down below
was carrying away,

when really 'All I want
is you to want me' was
all you wanted me to say.

# Winter Burial

*i.m. Liam Brady*

Twin jet trails crossing the sky;
here's us frozen in the lake of time
and up there God goes blithely skating by.

## Stradivarius

Spruce top, maple back and neck,
and willow for the blocks, the stops and stays
that hold this highly polished, gold-injected
cloud-mirror miracle in shape —

as if, before a note is ever played,
before it once exhales a single tone,
before its slender round full-scale attention
is ever oh so delicately brought to bear

on one withdrawing or advancing motion,
like the woods before the wind comes up full tilt,
the keel that's slowly weathered by the ocean,
the music's already listening to itself.

# Cakes

*i.m. Sheila & Betty Delany*

Those freshly baked cakes
cooling on the windowsill
forty years ago, *bejakers,*
and not cold still.

# Beetle

Little beetle,
      spinning on your back
           like a mad clock,

with a twig
      I flip you over
           and set you off

to work,
      to work you go
           in the family plot.

# Nebula

After winter drew up its raft
of bone and wrack and shadow
along the shoreline;

after the moon's pale eye
peered deeper into the garden's
breeze-block soul;

after the smoke-stacks filled with grief
and the stray cats gathered
on the one flat roof for miles

to keen their loss — chairs face-down
on the kitchen table, dishes stacked
on newsprint shelves,

brushes in hand as the dawn came up
between us we raised
a nebula of dust motes,

stopping to admire it,
as the gods are wont to do,
before setting off for home.

# Cutlery

A hill and a long road
leading up it, and a woman
sat up in a cushioned chair
in front of her house, watching —
you can see it in her eyes —
for some approach,

maybe that of a man
to whom she will speak
with the fearlessness of age
of the deeds of her life,
the events of her heart,
of the night, decades ago already,
when her husband, barely in
from the fields, washed his hands,
sat down there and fell asleep at table
breaking bread —

no warning,
no hint,
no premonition ...
time and timelessness,
the table just laid, the knife
still gripped in his hand,
the blade dipped in light.

# 'Lighthouse 1'

*after a painting by John Shinnors*

Darkness repeats
endlessly. Light
is always new.

# The Tune

*i.m. Pádraig McGrane*

Half of the evening
he sat in the kitchen
playing that tune

'Banish Misfortune'
(or 'The Spanish Man's Daughter'?
hard to be sure)

barely touching his drink
between cooker and sink
like a monk in a cell

set free by the roll
and the rise and the fall
of some shape-shifting spell

with its endless inventions
and half-baked intentions
till he came up for breath

and some boy in a wig
called for 'The Monaghan Jig' —
and we'd lost him again

# My Neighbour's Hand

Sudden laughter,
stuttering indignation,
but most of all
I loved the young girl's hand
my elderly neighbour
would slip into mine

those times she stopped me
on the topmost stair
to rail and rage
against the tyranny of landlords,
the liberal agenda,
the barbarism of our time —

that small hand independently
nestling into mine,
uncoiling, almost weightless —
like a leaf or spore
or butterfly descended
out of Heaven, I might have said,

had I even once acknowledged
its gossamer touch,
brought to mind the week she died
by her treasure trove of sacred things,
each one painstakingly wrapped
in its patina of dust.

# Oracle

Some claim helium from deep in the earth
leaking slowly up into the cave
gave the Pythia her unearthly voice

and her authority. But imagine this:
some high-pitched '70s disco band
or a gaggle of kids at the back of class,

singing like chipmunks, given the power
to decide whether an emissary should live
or die, some boatload of hotheads be sent

to sort out in their usual style — high-pitched
whooping, blood-curdling screams —
which local row might persist for a thousand years.


2.

In the late 1970s I recorded my father
for an advert he thought to broadcast to the town
on an old tape player and battered speaker

hung out on his Main Street shopfront.
'Pilgrimage to Lourdes'. It didn't help
that it was thirteen minutes long

and his dentures whistled as he spoke,
promising adventure and as much good food
"as would sink a battleship". We laughed at that,

at him, for days. Now, another miracle,
thirty years on, a decade since his death,
I listen to him speak of "rooming arrangements"

and "the language barrier", all the while
swallowing and coughing, and this time I laugh
through tears. And feel my own voice break.

# Obituary

His heart had four chambers where turf smoke tumbled.
His eyes filled with sky, like the pools in the yard.
His feet were the stones you hit with a shovel
when digging potatoes. His shoulders were hard.

He was the uncle we seldom encountered,
my father's reflection going unseen
between cow shed and creamery. His love, unexpected,
moved with the slow step of a man in a dream:

a dream among animals, a dream under stars,
a dream with, at best, two or three songs to name it,
a pint the odd evening, what passed for a car,
a few biscuits, the transistor, his bachelor gamut
of feelings expressed in the bark of his dog,
wind through the hayloft, those fields under fog.

# Night Walk

*for Gaetano Tranchino*


A man and his dog go walking in the evening
to where the street lights end, to the edge of town.
Under its full green sail they find the woodlands waiting.
The dog runs up and back then stands his ground.

And ah, the waves slip out and in, and in and out,
and on a sea of stars the full moon floats.
And oh, the swaying of the whispering trees
as if they dream of one day being boats.

## Sugimoto's 'Cabot Street Cinema, Massachusetts' (1978)

It's that celebrated cinema interior,
the seats all empty and the screen itself
glowing like the doorway to another world.

The photographer, it turns out,
sat and waited ninety minutes
until everyone he could see around him —
the kids with their buckets of popcorn,
the lovers holding hands,
the gaggle of teens and pre-teens
all giggles at the dashing hero's
every smouldering turn —
all of them vanished,

the long shutter setting
leaving only that screen,
brilliant and blank,
the light at the end of the tunnel,
the mouth of the cave.

# A Winter Blessing

*for Nobuaki Tochigi*

Since early evening snow has held us
spellbound at our windows,
erasing our plans, the world itself,
flake by innocuous flake.

'Letters sent from heaven'
the physicist Nakaya called them,
the snow crystals he grew and studied
in Hokkaido before the war,
his camera revealing
miraculous detail
in this deep and wide-thrown
blanket of forgetting.

Across the way, a light goes on
in a room that seems to float
in empty space. Snow
forgets, obliterates, subtracts
(by adding to), yet all the while
asks that we consider
the finer details
of who we are,
of what it is we rely upon
and love — at once
gift and theft, precious
and insubstantial,
and always new,

new as the world the caveman saw
when nothingness flared a moment
on his arm and vanished,

or the king waking up
in his stout-walled castle
impregnable from every direction
but above.

# Three Lines for Leland

A housefly settles
on the still end of my pen:
haiku counterweight.

# Lovers

*after the painting by Gustav Klimt*


The world's a grim and dark and deadly place,
but break it to us gently, Father Time;
let joy sing out when she first sees his face,
his heart-beat skip and trip, his breast inflate,
her pupils rapidly dilate, their postures rhyme;
let them climb out of the river of their fate
to lie and dream together side by side;
leave them this to treasure, this to constellate,
when all else under Heaven passes or collides.

# The Butterfly Farm

*i.m. Danny Rogers*

He wanted, he said, to leave us
a butterfly farm. The cottage
in Three Castles, though long since abandoned,
with a little work might become
a symbol of hope, a beacon
around which friends could gather
after he'd gone.

But life, as it tends to do,
had plans of its own: busy elsewhere
with the distractions of love,
with jokes to tell, adventures
to embellish, there were always
more pressing options
to be explored. And in the end,

though he talked of it often,
nothing was ever done:
the cottage fell into ruin,
weeds pushed up through everything,
and, needing no further encouragement,
like dancers at a country fair
in due course the butterflies appeared.

Lightning Source UK Ltd.
Milton Keynes UK
UKOW040120231012

200987UK00001B/25/P

9 781906 614553